50 Fun and Interesting Facts about the _Republican Party_

Immanuel Paine

"We will make America strong again. We will make America proud again. We will make America safe again. **And we will make America great again.**"

-Donald J. Trump

FACT 1:

MAGA stands for
"Make America Great Again"
And with Donald J. Trump as
our President, we will!

FACT 2:

The first Republican

President was

Abraham Lincoln.

He was the 16th President of

the United States.

He served this great nation

between 1861 to 1865.

FACT 3:

The Republican Party was founded in 1854 by **Freedom Loving Americans.**

FACT 4:

Ronald Reagan, a very popular Republican president, was an actor before entering politics. His nickname in Hollywood was "The Gipper," inspired by his role as George Gipp in the film "Knute Rockne, All American."

FACT 5:

The Republican Party is
sometimes referred to as the
GOP, which stands for the
Grand Old Party, a
nickname coined in the
1870s.

FACT 6:

The Republican Party's mascot is the **elephant**, and it was first associated in a political cartoon by **Thomas Nast** in Harper's Weekly in 1874.

FACT 7:

During his 1984 reelection campaign, President Reagan's optimistic message was encapsulated in the slogan **"It's Morning Again in America."**

FACT 8:

The **teddy bear** is named after Republican President Teddy Roosevelt.

FACT 9:

President Ronald Reagan was
known to enjoy
jelly beans, and he had a jar
of them on his desk.

FACT 10:

President Donald Trump was the host of the TV show **"The Apprentice"** and became known for his catchphrase "You're fired!"

If only we can do that with some of our Country's politicians!

FACT 11:

The Republican Party

supports

the Second Amendment

and the rights of individuals

to bear arms.

FACT 12:

The legendary actor and filmmaker **Clint Eastwood** has been a longtime Republican and supported various Republican candidates.

FACT 13:

Republican George H.W. Bush, the 41st President, was a **World War II veteran.**

FACT 14:

Before becoming President,
George W. Bush
co-owned the
**Texas Rangers baseball
team** from 1989 to 1998.

FACT 15:

Calvin Coolidge, the 30th President and a Republican, received **a pygmy hippopotamus named Billy** as a gift.

FACT 16:

The Republican Party has
always cared about Freedom.
Ronald Reagan famously said
**"Mr. Gorbachev, Tear
Down This Wall!"**

FACT 17:

On his 90th birthday, President George H.W. Bush celebrated by **skydiving**, showcasing his adventurous spirit.

FACT 18:

Republican Herbert Hoover, the 31st President, was an accomplished **geologist and mining engineer** before entering politics.

FACT 19:

The Americans with Disabilities Act (ADA) was signed into law by President George H.W. Bush in 1990, prohibiting discrimination against individuals with disabilities in various aspects of public life.

FACT 20:

The Republican Party is known for its support of **free-market capitalism**, emphasizing limited government intervention in the economy.

FACT 21:

The Republican Party has had a variety of campaign slogans over the years, including **"A Time for Choosing"** and **"It's Morning Again in America."**

FACT 22:

The Republican Party played
a significant role in passing
the **19th Amendment**
in 1920, giving women the
right to vote.

FACT 23:

Republicans are the ultimate casting director. For example, they have appointed three Justices: **Sandra Day O'Connor, Antonin Scalia, and Anthony Kennedy**.

FACT 24:

Republicans tend to advocate for **free-market principles**, believing that competition and entrepreneurship drive **economic innovation and prosperity**.

FACT 25:

Calvin Coolidge was the first sitting President to deliver a **radio address nationally**, showcasing the potential of the medium for reaching the public.

FACT 26:

President Ronald Reagan was a **WINNER!**

In the 1980 Election, Ronald Reagan defeated Jimmy Carter. Reagan won in a landslide, with 484 Electoral College votes. Jimmy only won 49!

And in the 1984 Election, Ronald Reagan won against Democrat Walter Mondale. Reagan won 525 Electoral College votes. Mondale only won 13!

FACT 27:

President Richard Nixon had a **bowling alley** installed in the White House basement, where he enjoyed practicing his bowling skills.

FACT 28:

President Donald Trump signed the **First Step Act** in 2018, a bipartisan criminal justice reform bill aimed at reducing recidivism and improving prison conditions.

FACT 29:

President Ronald Reagan's economic policies, known as **Reaganomics**, aimed to reduce government intervention and stimulate economic growth through tax cuts.

FACT 30:

The Republican Party is aligned with conservative values, including a focus on **traditional family values, religious freedom, and pro-life stances.**

FACT 31:

President Trump
established the
United States Space Force
in 2019 as the sixth branch of
the U.S. military.

Go USA!

FACT 32:

President Richard Nixon made a historic phone call to astronauts **Neil Armstrong and Buzz Aldrin** while they were on the **moon** during the **Apollo 11 mission**.

FACT 33:

President Richard Nixon was the first President to visit **China**, marking a significant moment in international relations.

FACT 34:

President Dwight D. Eisenhower, the 34th President, was a **Five-Star General** during World War II before becoming President.

FACT 35:

President Teddy Roosevelt installed a **boxing ring** in the White House and regularly sparred with professional boxers.

FACT 36:

President Ronald Reagan's ranch was initially called a different name until a local elementary school won a naming contest, renaming it the **"Reagan Ranch."**

FACT 37:

Republicans care about
school choice.
They have advocated for
voucher programs and
charter schools.

Parents should have a voice
in children's education!

FACT 38:

Paul Ryan, the Republican Speaker of the House from 2015 to 2019 became the **youngest Speaker** at age 45 since James Blaine in 1869.

FACT 39:

Republicans care about our Second Amendment. In the ruling of District of Columbia v. Heller in 2008, the Supreme Court affirmed the **right to possess firearms for self-defense within the home.**

FACT 40:

President Theodore Roosevelt expanded the **National Park System**, creating five national parks, 18 national monuments, and initiating conservation efforts.

FACT 41:

The phrase **"speak softly and carry a big stick"** is often associated with Theodore Roosevelt and encapsulates his approach to foreign policy.
This approach became known as the **"Big Stick" diplomacy**

FACT 42:

Republican administrations
are pro-business.
The Tax Cuts and Jobs Act,
during President Trump's
administration, reduced
corporate taxes, with the aim
of encouraging
business investment and
expansion.

FACT 43:

Republicans advocate for **limited government intervention in individuals' lives**, promoting personal freedoms and individual responsibility.

FACT 44:

Camp David is named after Republican President Dwight D. Eisenhower's grandson!

FACT 45:

President Trump beat Hilary
Clinton in the 2016 Election.

**Make America Great
Again!**

FACT 46:

The Republican Party is
associated with the **red**.
This began during the 2000
Election between
Bush and Gore.

FACT 47:

President Dwight D. Eisenhower played a crucial role in the space race by creating **NASA** in response to the Soviet Union's early achievements in **space exploration**.

FACT 48:

In 1989, a board game called **"Trump: The Game"** was released, where players could experience the **excitement of real estate deals.**

This game was inspired by President Donald Trump.

FACT 49:

President Teddy Roosevelt

was the **youngest person**

ever to become President at

the age of 42.

FACT 50:

The 2024 Election will be the most important election for the Republican Party!